Life of Fred

Goldfish

Life of Fred

Goldfish

Stanley F. Schmidt, Ph.D.

Polka Dot Publishing

ISBN: 978-1-937032-00-5

Library of Congress Catalog Number: 2011915652
Printed and bound in the United States of America

Polka Dot Publishing   Reno, Nevada

To order copies of books in the Life of Fred series,

visit our website PolkaDotPublishing.com

Questions or comments? Email Polka Dot Publishing at lifeoffred@yahoo.com

First printing

for Goodness' sake

or as J.S. Bach—who was
never noted for his plain
English—often expressed it:

Ad Majorem Dei Gloriam
(to the greater glory of God)

If you happen to spot an error that the author, the publisher, and the printer missed, please let us know with an email to: lifeoffred@yahoo.com

As a reward, we'll email back to you a list of all the corrections that readers have reported.

HOW MANY TIMES DO YOU READ THIS BOOK?

Once? A child reading the nineteen chapters and doing all the exercises will learn about a third of what is in this book.

They "get it" and then they "forget it." That's just the way human beings are. We are not cameras or tape recorders.

Do kids ever watch the same movie more than once? Of course. You might hear one child tell another, *"The Pirates of Kansas* is my favorite movie. I have seen it five times."

They start to memorize every scene. They learn all the dialog.

How do teachers know the material much better than their students? They have gone over the same material many times.

In Chapter 18, we will read that 10 centimeters of dental floss is about four inches. How many readers, when they get to Chapter 19, will remember that? Not that many.

It is only when you play with an idea that it begins to "stick." And there are many ways to play with an idea.

WAYS TO PLAY

1. Take it into the rest of your life. The back of an adult hand—is that four inches? It's 10 cm.

2. Teach it. I, your author, have taught this material many times and know it deeply. Many parents have reported to me that their children talk about Fred at the dinner table. What are they doing? They are *teaching* it. And the result is that they learn it.

3. Your older child can read *Fred* to a younger sibling.

4. One calculus teacher wrote to me recently. She has her students rewrite parts of the *Life of Fred: Calculus* story with new adventures for

Fred that teach the same calculus. She included a large collection of their stories for me to read. The students were evidently having a lot of fun—and in the process, learning a lot of calculus.

There is a dirty word for all these Ways to Play. It is . . .

The path to real learning

I have tried to make learning as much fun as possible. Enjoyment really helps learning. But one essential element of learning is repetition. That's a part of practice.

Do you remember potty training? How many kids are perfect after the first lesson?

Pistol Pete Maravich—one of the greats in basketball—would head off to the gym on Saturday mornings. He would pick at particular spot on the court and shoot baskets from that one spot . . . until the gym closed at night. The next Saturday he would pick a different spot on the court.

Most people would rather spend their Saturdays doing fun stuff, and most people can't play basketball like Pistol Pete.

THIS BOOK

One question I've often received from moms is, "If my child already knows the addition tables, where do I start in the Life of Fred Elementary Series?"

Each of the books in this series contains much more than just the addition and multiplication facts.*

For example, *Life of Fred: Cats* includes discussions of Ursa Major (Big Bear), Commutative, Asterism, Vowels, Cardinality of a Set, Loud Talkers, Hiring Freeze, One Quarter, Numerals vs. Numbers, Counting by Threes, Hoodwinked, Finding Patterns, Sheet Music for "Happy", Four Basic Emotions, Right Angles, Quarter and Half Notes, Obligate Carnivores, Adjectives and Verbs, Carbohydrates, a Quarter to Three, the Mariana Trench, 5280 Feet in a Mile, Ferdinand Magellan's Trip, What *Pacific* Means, Bacteria, Rabies in 300 B.C., Treating Cat Scratches, Capital Letters Start Sentences, Five Vowel Words: May, Me, Might, Mow, Mut, Twenty-Two English Words That Don't Contain a Vowel: *By, Cry, . . . , Tryst*, and *Why*, Numbers Expressed as Hundreds, Tens and Ones, Sexagesimal and Decimal Systems, Numbers that Add to 13, Morse Code, Four Major Oceans of the World, Centuries, Centenarians, and Centurions, Homonyms, Square Feet, Prepositional Phrases, 71 English Prepositions, Volume, One Meter, the Three Countries of the World that Don't Primarily Use the Metric System. What Mathematicians Do, Prime Numbers, and Less Than ($<$), among other things.

I urge those moms to start with *Life of Fred: Apples*. Besides learning a lot of material on a wide variety of subjects, this will give the child a pleasant way to practice—the path to real learning.

HOW THIS BOOK IS ORGANIZED

Just like the previous books in the series: Each chapter is about six pages. At the end of each chapter is a Your Turn to Play.

Have a paper and pencil handy before you sit down to read.

Each Your Turn to Play consists of about three or four questions. Have your child write out the answers—not just mentally answer them.

After all the questions are answered, then take a peek at my answers that are given on the next page. At this point your child has *earned* the right to go on to the next chapter.

Don't just read the questions and look at the answers. Your child won't learn as much taking that shortcut.

---

* If you just wanted to learn that, a couple packs of flash cards would do the trick.

Contents

Chapter One
Which Pet?

A little noontime nap is rare for Fred. During the week he is teaching at KITTENS from 8 to 5. His weekends are usually so filled that taking a little snooze is impossible.

Today Fred discovered that a little nap can feel very good.

He slept for 40 minutes.

If his life included music or poetry, a nap could be considered the perfect caesura.*

12·40

His doll, Kingie, had been quietly painting while Fred slept. When Fred awoke, Kingie said, "I've been thinking. You got me from King of French Fries when you were only about four days old. We've been together a little over five years now."

"That's true," Fred said. "This is now my fifth February at KITTENS. The time has passed so quickly."

---

* seh-ZOO-rah A caesura is a pause—such as a break in a musical phrase, or in poetry in the middle of a line.

"What I was thinking," Kingie said, "was that during most of our time, we have not had any pets.

When you were one, we didn't have pets.

When you were two, we didn't have pets.

When you were three, we didn't have pets.

When you were four, we didn't have pets.

Now that you've turned five, you have turned pet crazy."

Fred shrugged his shoulders. "Maybe it is just a stage that five-year-olds go through. It's the I-need-a-pet stage."

Kingie asked, "Did you just make that up?"

Fred grinned. "I did. I've never read that in any book, but it sounds true. Don't kids sometimes go through an I-need-a-pet stage?"

"I wouldn't know," said Kingie. "I've never had kids."

Kingie went back to painting for a moment.

Fred got up and was putting away his sleeping bag.

Kingie began again, "The reason I brought up this pet business is because we have never had a happy time with pets."

"Didn't you like the butterflies?" Fred asked. They were quiet and pretty."

"Ha! Those stupid butterflies left those bugs on your desk. They were horrible," Kingie almost shouted.

"I thought they were cute" Fred said. "And besides, the butterflies didn't leave bugs. They left their eggs, which turned into friendly little caterpillars."

Kingie continued, "And then, after you had those bugs, you brought home a tiger!"

"It was just a little kitty," Fred said.

"Kitty!" Kingie yelled. "I saw the picture of its mother in the newspaper. That's why I built my fort. I needed to protect myself from your pet. And then you had 30 dogs! That was nuts. The only good pet we have had around here is that lovely mouse that you brought home from Edgewood."

Mama missing one of her cubs

"What mouse!" Now it was Fred's turn to shout. "I'm terrified of mice!"

Kingie explained to Fred that it had been in Fred's backpack. The mouse had explored

Kingie's fort while Fred slept. And then it got eaten by the obligate carnivore in the hallway.

So now they were caterpillarless, catless, dogless, and mouseless.*

The pets that Fred liked—butterflies, cats, dogs—were the ones that Kingie didn't like.

And the pet that Kingie liked—mouse—was the one that Fred didn't like.

Fred suggested, "We really need to find a pet that both of us like."

Kingie said, "Okay. But, first, let's list the pets that we don't want."

Kingie began the list. This is Kingie's handwriting.

Pets We Don't Want

1. No bugs

2. No cats

3. No dogs

Fred added in his handwriting . . .

4. No mice

5. Nothing that looks like a mouse. No rats. No gophers. No rodents. No moles. No hamsters.

---

* There really is no word like *caterpillarless*, etc. There are words like *homeless*, which Fred wasn't. He had a nice office to live in.

And there is *penniless*, which Fred currently is—or at least until his next paycheck, which will come at beginning of March.

Kingie added . . .

6. *No spiders*

7. *No moths*

8. *Nothing that crawls around on the ground. No bugs. No snakes. No worms. No beatles. No lizards.*

Fred added . . .

9. Nothing from a zoo. No hippos. No lions. No gorillas. No elephants.

Your Turn to Play

1. At the university, Fred teaches from 8 a.m. to 5 p.m. How many hours is that?

2. This is his fifth year at KITTENS. Is *fifth* a cardinal or an ordinal number?

3. Kingie told Fred, "When you were four, we didn't have pets." Is *four* a cardinal number or an ordinal number?

4. When Kingie and Fred were making their list of pets that they didn't want, Fred wrote **No elephants**. Why do you imagine he didn't want an elephant as a pet?

5. {bug, cat, dog} ∪ {bug, dog}

6. Find a value for x that makes this true: $x + 3 = 12$.

7. Find a value for y that makes this true: $2y = 10$.

 2y means the same as 2 times y.

 2y means the same as $2 \times y$.

 2y means the same as $y + y$.

. . . . ANSWERS . . . .

1. The elapsed time between 8 in the morning and 5 in the afternoon can be figured out in several different ways. My favorite way is:

first, from 8 to noon is $12 - 8 = 4$ hours,

second, from noon to 5 is 5 hours.

He teaches 4 hours in the morning and 5 hours in the afternoon. Each day he teaches for 9 hours.

2. *Fifth* is an ordinal number. The ordinal numbers are first, second, third, fourth, fifth, sixth, etc.

3. *Four* is a cardinal number. The cardinal numbers are used for counting the number of members of sets. The smallest cardinal number is zero.

The cardinality of { } is 0.

The cardinality of {8, 44, ☽} is 3.

4. There are many possible reasons. Here are some that I could think of:

✓ An elephant wouldn't fit very easily into Fred's office.

✓ It would cost a lot of money to feed an elephant.

✓ Fred didn't want to clean up after an elephant.

✓ It would be tough to get an elephant up the two flights of stairs to Fred's office.

5. {bug, cat, dog} ∪ {bug, dog} = {bug, cat, dog}

(Remember the spelling rule for sets: *Don't list a member more than once.* {bug, cat, dog, bug, dog} is not nice.)

6. $x + 3 = 12$ is true when x is 9.

7. $2y = 10$ is true when y is equal to 5.

Chapter Two
Manias

Fred and Kingie weren't done making their list of *Pets We Don't Want*. Kingie knew that he had to think hard. He didn't want to forget something.

vulture

"No vultures!" Kingie said. He was so glad he thought of that. That would have been an easy one to miss.

"No chickens," Fred said. "The eggs would be nice, but they would be messy in an office."

"No cattle!" Kingie said, and then he added, "And no other farm animals."

Fred knew that that included lambs.

Actually, Fred's urge to try farming was fading. When you are five years old, you go through a lot of different manias. One day you might be excited about farming. The next day you want to build things with little plastic bricks. The next day all you can think about is that new game that just came out.

Going crazy about the color purple one day, and thinking about being a movie star the next day are all a part of growing up.

Kingie remembered Fred's mania about getting a dog. He remembered the 30 dogs they had in Fred's office.

❀   ❀   ❀

small essay
Manias

Adults have manias. Several centuries ago many people in Holland went nuts about owning tulips. Some of them paid a year's wages for a single bulb.

Toads have passions. In the book *The Wind in the Willows*, Toad went crazy about automobiles.

Nations have manias. Some of which have unhappy endings.

❀   ❀   ❀

"And no birds of any kind," Kingie said. "All those birds you get in a pet store go 'Tweet! Tweet!' or 'Chirp! Chirp!' That noise is enough to drive anyone crazy. And, besides, cleaning out birdcages is a messy job."

"We could let our little birdie just fly around the office," Fred suggested.

"NO BIRDS!" Kingie shouted. "We would have an office to clean up instead of a cage."

Fred hadn't thought about that. He had just thought about how nice it would be to have a bird sitting on his shoulder as he studied math.

Important facts:
    Adult ostriches can weigh up to 340 pounds and be up to 9 feet tall.
    Fred weighs 37 pounds and is 3 feet tall.

    340 pounds > 37 pounds
    9 feet > 3 feet

    The National Geographic magazine states that kicks from an ostrich can kill a lion. It doesn't mention what it could do to a small KITTENS math professor.

It should also be noted . . .

The birds on the previous page were not **drawn to scale**. Owls are not as big as ostriches.

If the ostrich and the hummingbird were drawn to scale, they would look like this:

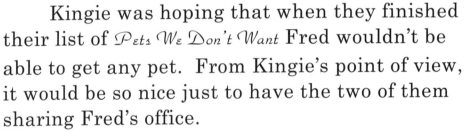

Kingie was hoping that when they finished their list of *Pets We Don't Want* Fred wouldn't be able to get any pet. From Kingie's point of view, it would be so nice just to have the two of them sharing Fred's office.

Just the two of us, Kingie thought. *We could be like two happy birds.*

pencil sketch of
Two Happy Birds

He began an oil painting to illustrate that thought. The first step was to make a pencil drawing. Some artists (and some mathematicians) use pencils and erasers because it makes it easier to make changes and corrections.

Two Happy Birds
by Kingie

Later that afternoon Kingie would complete his oil painting.

Your Turn to Play

1. It was 12:40 when Fred awoke from his nap. It was now 1:15. How long was it since he woke up?

2. Find a value of x that makes this true: 2x = 18.

3. Find a value of y that makes this true: 3y = 12.

4. What is one-half of 10?

    (That means what number added to itself gives you 10.)

5. What is one-half of 200?

6. What is the largest five-digit number?

7. Name the smallest one-digit number.

. . . . ANSWERS . . . .

1. From 12:40 to 1:00   20 minutes

    From 1:00 to 1:15   + 15 minutes

                                35 minutes

    It's 35 minutes from 12:40 to 1:15.

2. If x = 9, then 2x = 18.

3. If y = 4, then 3y = 12.   4 + 4 + 4 = 12

4. One-half of 10 is 5.   5 + 5 = 10

5. One-half of 200 is 100.   100 + 100 = 200

6. The largest five-digit number is 99,999.

7. The smallest one-digit number is 0.

A Row of Practice.

Cover the gray answers with a blank sheet of paper. Write your answers on your paper. Then after you have done the whole row, check your answers. *If your answers are not all correct, then get out a new sheet of paper and do this row again.*

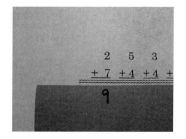

$$
\begin{array}{cccccc}
58 & 90 & 55 & 7 & 73 \\
+\ 47 & -\ 62 & +\ 87 & \times\ 2 & +\ 97 \\
\hline
105 & 28 & 142 & 14 & 170
\end{array}
$$

Chapter Three
Mail

The Saturday mail arrived. Fred sorted it. Most of the letters were for Kingie. Many were orders for his future paintings.

Fred got one piece of mail.

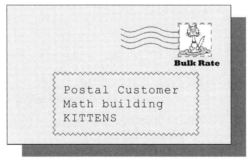

On the back of the envelope it was marked, "Personal and Confidential," and "To be opened by addressee only!"

That made Fred feel special.

He put three phone books on his chair so that he would be tall enough to sit at his desk.

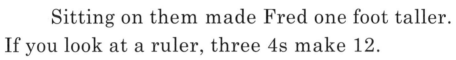

Each phone book was 4 inches thick.

Three of them together made 12 inches.

Three times four is twelve. $3 \times 4 = 12$.

Sitting on them made Fred one foot taller. If you look at a ruler, three 4s make 12.

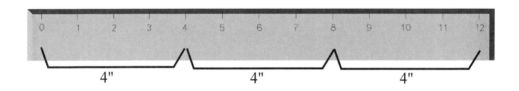

Fred sat at his desk. He carefully opened the envelope.

Fred put the ad in his pocket, gave Kingie a hug, and dashed out the door.

He ran down the hallway past the nine vending machines (four on one side and five on the other), down two flights of stairs, and off to 789 Lizard Lane.

Time Out!

Super important fact of life: **When you go nuts about something, your brain turns off.**

Fred had a mania about getting a pet. He absolutely, positively had to own an animal.

When you go crazy about something, you can become dumb as dirt.

Fred had read only one word in the letter. He read, "Pets."

small essay

What Fred Didn't See

#1. It was mailed at the bulk rate. How could the letter say that the grand opening was *today*? Bulk rate letters are not delivered on a particular day.

#2. How believable would it be that the "world's best pet store" was located somewhere in the middle of Kansas?

#3. If their "regular prices" were sky high, "half off" would not be a bargain.

#4. What does "lifetime guarantee" really mean?

Does it mean . . .

A. The pet is guaranteed as long as you are alive?

B. The pet is guaranteed as long as the pet is alive?

C. The store is guaranteeing that the pet you buy is really healthy?

D. The store is guaranteeing that you will be happy with the pet?

E. The store is guaranteeing that if you buy a dog, that it is really a dog.

#5. Fred read, "Cheapest prices on the block!" but it didn't occur to him that **Pets—You Bet!** is the only store on the block.

#6. Fred didn't notice that name in the lower right corner of the ad. Some people are honest, and you can really trust them. Do they say that about you? They don't say that about C. C. Coalback.

Fred ran past the Archimedes building where he teaches his math classes, past the university chapel, and past the tennis courts.

When he got to the point where Tangent Road, Newton Steet, and Archimedes Lane all meet, he realized one small thing. He had no idea where Lizard Lane was.

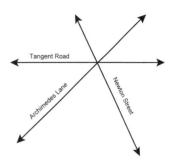

Lines are **concurrent** if they all meet at the same point.

It couldn't have been on the KITTENS campus. He knew every part of the campus.

It must be in some part of the town that he had never been in.

Your Turn to Play

1. 789 Lizard Lane was pretty easy to remember. The digits—7, 8, and 9—were consecutive numbers. *Lizard Lane* was alliterative. (Alliterative = words starting with the same sound, such as Fred's fine photographs.)

Suppose you were designing a new city and you got to name each place on the map. (Did you ever realize that somebody sometime in the last 500 years named the street you live on?)

You could make all the names alliterative if you wanted to. If you had a street, you could name it Silly Street or Strawberry Street.

Now it's your turn. If you had an avenue, what might you name it.

2. Give an alliterative name for a boulevard.

3. For a court.

4. For a drive.

5. What is one-half of 20?

······**ANSWERS**·······

1. We want an alliterative name for an avenue. Your answer may be different than mine. I thought of Apple Avenue, Alexander Avenue, Avaricious Avenue (avaricious means greedy), Automatic Avenue, Average Avenue, and Ascending Avenue (for a street that goes uphill).

2. Your answer may be different than mine. I thought of Betty Boulevard, Butterfly Boulevard, and Boo-Boo Boulevard.

3. Candy Court, Kitty Court (for alliteration, the words have to start with the same *sound*, not necessarily with the same letter), Kidney Court, and Cozy Court.

4. Darlene Drive, Ducky Drive, Daisy Drive, Descending Drive and **DRIPPY DRIVE**.

5. One-half of 20 is 10.

$$\begin{array}{r} 10 \\ +\ 10 \\ \hline 20 \end{array}$$

A Row of Practice. *Do the whole row before you look at the answers.*

57	435	7	4	535
+ 98	− 8	× 2	× 3	+ 778
155	427	14	12	1313

Chapter Four
Map

Fred ran back to his office—past the tennis courts, the university chapel, and the Archimedes building. He ran up two flights of stairs, down the hallway past the nine vending machines (six on one side and three on the other*) and into his office.

He sat on the three four-inch phone books** and opened a desk drawer. In it were some Farmer's Nachos, two sandwiches, a slice of birthday cake, a dish of ice cream, a loaf of bread, a dried out peach, and a map.

3 four-inch phone books = 12 inches

He took the peach out of the drawer and looked at it. It was small as an eyeball, as hard as a baseball, and had as many wrinkles as an unmade bed.

---

* Someone moved one of the machines!

** Who drew this picture? It certainly wasn't Kingie He would know how to draw things to scale. In this drawing, Fred looks shorter than the three phone books. That would make him less than one foot tall. Fred is really three feet tall.

Time Out!

Similes (SIM-eh-ease) can make your writing come alive. A simile (SIM-eh-lee) is a comparison using *like* or *as*.

Do you remember the simile in the previous chapter *dumb as dirt*? That is much more memorable than just *dumb*.

Someday you may write a book. Or you may write a speech or even a love letter.

love letter without similes:

Dear You,
    You are cute. I like you.
         Me

love letter with similes:

Dear You,
    You are cute as a button. I like you like a morning at Disneyland.
         Me

The peach also smelled like unwashed socks. Fred put it back into the drawer "for later." He took out the map.

Lizard Lane was east of KITTENS.

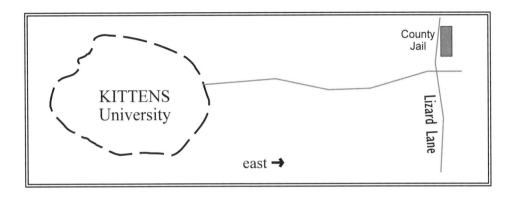

The pet store is on the same road as the county jail, Fred thought. *That jail is probably where they took Coalback and his sister after the police arrested them.*

It never occurred to Fred to wonder how Coalback could be in jail and opening the Pets—You Bet! pet store at the same time.

Any of these might be true:

A) Coalback may have posted bail. (Translation: The court set Coalback free until he had to appear to stand trial. He had to put up money—post bail—to guarantee that he would show up for trial. If he didn't show up for trial, he would lose the money.)

B) He could have already gone to trial and been found innocent. This is hard to believe for two reasons: (1) He was guilty, and (2) It is Saturday and the justice system does not operate that quickly. Trials can sometimes take weeks or even months.

C) He had escaped.

D) He had been pardoned by the governor who happened to be a close friend of his.*

---

* Can you pardon someone before he has been tried and convicted? Yes.

    History, if it's taught right, can be almost as much fun as math. Learning about history should not be just memorizing a bunch of dates.

    Perhaps, the most famous pardon in the last hundred years was when Ford pardoned Nixon in 1974.

    Nixon was president. Ford was vice president. Nixon did some bad stuff. He resigned, and Ford took over as president in August. In September, Ford went on television and announced a full pardon for everything that Nixon "has committed or may have committed" during his presidency.

    Ford stated, ". . . I feel that Richard Nixon and his loved ones have suffered enough. . . ." At this point Nixon had never been arrested or formally accused of anything. If you steal a car and the police come to arrest you, you could tell them, "I feel I have suffered enough."

    Thirty-two years later, the New York Times (December 29, 2006) reported that when Ford was still vice president, Nixon's chief of staff handed Ford two pieces of paper: one was a description of the president's power to pardon and the second was a blank pardon form. How strange. Ford wasn't president. He was just vice president.

    Then six weeks later, Nixon decided to resign.

    In 2004 Ford told a reporter, "I had no hesitancy about granting the pardon, because I felt that we had this relationship and that I didn't want to see my real friend have the stigma." (*stigma* = guilty stain)

    Historians don't know for certain. Did Ford pardon Nixon because they were buddies? Did Ford pardon Nixon because they had made a deal: Nixon would resign which would make Ford the president if Ford agreed to pardon Nixon?

    The nice thing about math is that you can get answers.

Your Turn to Play

1. If you can count by 5s, you know that three 5s are equal to 15: *five, ten, fifteen.*

    Three times five equals 15.

    $3 \times 5 = 15$.

Here are 3 rows, with 5 dots in each row:

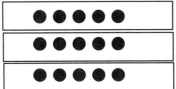 $3 \times 5 = 15$

Here are 5 columns with 3 dots in each column:

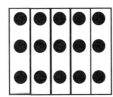 $5 \times 3 = 15$

So 3×5 gives the same answer as 5×3.

Your turn to play: Show that $3 \times 6 = 18$ and $6 \times 3 = 18$.

2. It's fun to write similes. Complete each of these:

Her smile was as bright as_____.

His eyes were red like_____.

Reading is as enjoyable as_____.

· · · · · · · **ANSWERS** · · · · · · ·

1. Here are 3 rows, with 6 dots in each row:

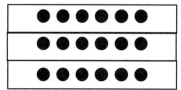

$3 \times 6 = 18$

Here are 6 columns with 3 dots in each column:

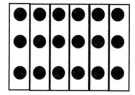

$6 \times 3 = 18$

So $3 \times 6 = 18$ and $6 \times 3 = 18$.

2. Your answers may be different than mine.

Her smile was as bright as snow, as sunshine, as a new dime, as life itself, as a 5000-watt light bulb.

His eyes were red like cherry tomatoes, like stop lights, like red marbles. (He apparently had been crying a lot.)

Reading is as enjoyable as pizza!

Chapter Five
To the Pet Store

Nothing could stop Fred now. He knew where the pet store was located. He was wearing his jogging shoes. Today was the grand opening day.

He gave Kingie a hug. Kingie handed him the list of *Pets We Don't Want* to make sure that Fred didn't get so excited that he would bring home a bug or a cat or a dog.

It was Kingie's secret hope that the list was so complete that Fred couldn't wouldn't be able to get any animal.

Fred headed down the hallway past the nine vending machines (five on one side and four on the other*) down the two flights of stairs, and east toward Lizard Lane.

When he was halfway to the pet store he realized that he didn't have any money with him. He ran back to his office.

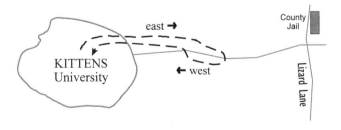

---

* Someone moved one of the machines again.

"I forgot my money," Fred said to Kingie.

"You don't have any money," Kingie reminded Fred. "Don't you remember? Coalback stole every cent you had."

Fred frowned. He had forgotten that. Fred wasn't very good at holding grudges against anyone.

Kingie lent him some money from his art sales.

Fred looked at the clock. It was 25 minutes to three. He hoped that the pet store wouldn't close early on its grand opening day.

2:35 p.m.

As Fred left his office, Kingie handed him a revised list of *Pets We Don't Want*. He had added one more thing: *And no animals that breathe!* That would make sure that Fred wouldn't get *any* pet.

True Fact
When dolls write up Christmas lists,
they rarely ask for pets.

As Fred ran to the store, he imagined that **Pets—You Bet!** might have sold all the good pets before he got there.

He ran even faster.

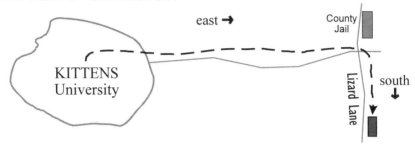

Fred was running at the rate of 3 blocks per minute. He ran for 6 minutes. In the old days (before *Life of Fred: Goldfish*) you would have had to add up:

3 blocks
3 blocks
3 blocks
3 blocks
3 blocks
+ 3 blocks

he ran 18 blocks.

Now since we know the $6 \times 3 = 18$, our work is much shorter.

The whole point of math is *to make our work easier.* Before you learned to add, you would have to count on your fingers and toes to know that $8 + 9 = 17$. Now you instantly know it.

Fred had arrived.

He rushed inside and asked the clerk, "Do you have any pets left for sale?"

She answered, "You bet. We have lots of them."

She pointed to a row of dogs.

Fred wanted to buy all of them, but dogs were on the *Pets We Don't Want* list.

 "We have one cat," she said.

Fred knew there was something really wrong with that cat. He knew that cats were obligate carnivores.

"We have three lovely lambs that you are sure to like. They are $26 each."

Fred did a quick computation. $3 \times 26 = \$78$.

Here's how it's done:

$$\begin{array}{r} \overset{1}{2}6 \\ \times\ \ 3 \\ \hline 78 \end{array}$$

In words: 3 times 6 is 18.

Write down the 8, and carry the one.

3 times 2 is 6, plus the one, equals 7.

Your Turn to Play

1. Give it a try. $3 \times 14 = ?$

2. We showed that $3 \times 5 = 15$ with dots:

 $3 \times 5 = 15$

Draw some dots to show that $3 \times 3 = 9$.

3. Fred had borrowed $100 from Kingie. If he spent $78 for Lambert, Lilly, and Lucy, how much would he have left?

.... ANSWERS ....

1. $\overset{1}{1}4$ 3 times 4 is 12.

    × 3   Write down the 2 and carry the one.

     42   3 times 1 is 3, plus the one, equals 4.

2. $3 \times 3 = 9$

3. $1\overset{9}{\cancel{0}}{}^{1}0$

    − 78

     22   Fred would have $22 left.

A Row of Practice.   *Do the whole row before you look at the answers.*

44	584	7	3	634
+ 89	− 7	× 2	× 3	+ 856
133	577	14	9	1490

Chapter Six
Selecting a Pet

F red had a fistful of dollars. He didn't know that you are not supposed to wave your money around. Most people are honest, but there are some that are not.

"How much money do you have to spend on a lovely pet?" the clerk asked.

The clerk looked vaguely familiar to Fred. He had seen her somewhere before.

Hint: This is what she looked like before getting a wig, a new dress and earrings.

She was Coalback's sister and was wearing a disguise. She didn't want anyone to recognize her.

Fred told her, "I have a hundred dollars."

"That's just perfect," she said. "It just happens that all of our pets are on sale today. Any pet is $100.*" Coalback's

---

* If Fred had said, "$83," then all the pets would have been on sale for $83.

sister was up to her old tricks. And Fred, who was always trusting, never seemed to learn.

Fred explained that there were certain pets that he couldn't buy: **no bugs, no cats, no dogs, no mice, nothing that looks like a mouse (such as rats, gophers, rodents, moles or hamsters), no spiders, no moths, nothing that crawls around on the ground, nothing from the zoo, no vultures, no chickens, no cattle, no other farm animals, no birds, and no animal that breathes.**

"That narrows things down a bit," she said. "We have a lovely dead coyote* that we found outside the store. We guarantee that it doesn't breathe."

Example of a non-dead coyote

Fred shook his head. A coyote was too much like a dog. He was also thinking of getting a live pet rather than a dead one.

Fred looked at four animals that were in the pet store and played the game of Which of These Is Not Like the Others.

dead coyote

---

* It's not spelled anything like how it's pronounced. ki-YO-tee. If I were first learning how to read, I would think that *coyote* would be pronounced co-YOAT.

At first, Fred thought that the cat was not like the others. It was the only obligate carnivore.

Then Fred thought that the bird was not like the others. It was the only one that laid eggs.

Then Fred thought that the dinosaur was not like the others. It was extinct.

Then he thought the coyote was not like the others. It was the only one that had been recently alive and was now dead.

He wondered how they could have a dinosaur in the pet store. He looked closely at the tail. The dinosaur was made out of rubber.

While Fred was playing his Which of These Is Not Like the Other game, the clerk went into the back room to talk with her brother.

She was desperate. She explained to C. C. Coalback that this kid had $100 to spend, but he had a long list pets that he couldn't buy. She repeated all the things that Fred had told her.

"That's easy," he said. "I'll take care of him."

He headed out to see Fred and get his money.

Fred was playing his game. He thought of four numbers:

7   36   8   ½

Which one was not like the others?

7 is the only odd number in the group.

36 is the only two-digit number in the group.

8 is the only one that is a homonym ("sounds alike"). 8 and *ate*.

½ is the only fraction in the group.

C. C. walked up to Fred and smiled. It was a slithery smile.*

"I hear you'd like to get a nice pet," he began.

Fred nodded and held up $100.

"My sister tells me that you say no bugs, no cats, no dogs, no mice, nothing that looks like a mouse (such as rats, gophers, rodents, moles or hamsters), no spiders, no moths, nothing that crawls around on the ground, nothing from the zoo, no vultures, no chickens, no cattle, no other farm animals, no birds, and no animal that breathes.

---

* Snakes don't walk, hop, or fly. They slither.

"That's correct," Fred said.

"What do you mean by *no bugs*?"

Fred explained, "My doll doesn't like to see any creepy-crawly things."

"So if I can get you something that's alive that isn't creepy-crawly that would scare your doll and isn't a cat, a dog, a mouse, or anything that looks like a mouse (such as rats, gophers, rodents, moles or hamsters), a spider, a moth, or anything that crawls around on the ground, from the zoo, or is a bird, or another farm animal, then you are telling me you would buy it?"

Fred thought for a minute and said, "Yes, as long as it doesn't breathe air."

Your Turn to Play

1. Let's play Which of These Is Not Like the Others. Find a reason which each of these is not like the other three.

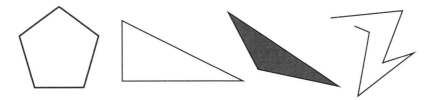

2.   25
    $\times\ 3$

3. If tomorrow will be Wednesday, what day was yesterday?

.......ANSWERS ....

1. Much of mathematics is learning to see patterns in things. When you are first learning to count by twos (2, 4, 6, 8, 10, 12 . . .), you may notice that every other natural number is even: 1, *2*, 3, *4*, 5, *6*, 7, *8*. . . .

Later, in algebra, if you are told that x is an odd number, you will be able to predict that x + 1 must be an even number.

This is the only figure with five sides.

It is also the only regular polygon. (Polly-GONE)

(regular polygon = all sides have some length and all angles are equal)

This is the only figure with a right angle.

This is the only one that is filled in.

This is the only one that couldn't be filled in.

The two "ends" are not connected.

This is not a polygon.

Your answers to question one may have been different than mine.

2. $\overset{1}{2}5$ 3 times 5 is 15.

    × 3   Write down the 5 and carry the one.

    75   3 times 2 is 6, plus the one, equals 7.

3. If tomorrow will be Wednesday, today is Tuesday, and yesterday was Monday.

Chapter Seven
Zillions of Pets

Coalback wanted to be sure that all the terms of their agreement were clear. He asked Fred if he understood that all the pets at Pets—You Bet! are $100. Fred understood that.

Coalback said that he had pets that fit Fred's criteria: no bugs, no cats, no dogs, no mice, nothing that looks like a mouse (such as rats, gophers, rodents, moles or hamsters), no spiders, no moths, nothing that crawls around on the ground, nothing from the zoo, no vultures, no chickens, no cattle, no other farm animals, no birds, and no animal that breathes and that were alive. Coalback promised that he wouldn't give Fred a dead coyote.

Coalback explained that the pets he had in mind didn't have any lungs so they couldn't breathe. Fred said that that was exactly what he wanted.

Fred had a mania. All he could think of was *I want a pet.*

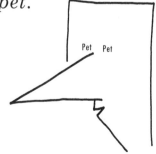

Kids with manias often pester their parents, saying, "I want a Rag-A-Fluffy doll. All

my friends have Rag-A-Fluffy dolls. I need one!
Buy one for me."

Fred didn't have parents. There was no
one there to tell Fred that he was making a big
mistake.

Fred said, "I'll buy it. I don't care what
color it is or what size it is."

Coalback took out his handkerchief and
blew his nose. He handed the handkerchief to
Fred and took the $100.

With a wiggly smile, Coalback said, "There
you are, my little man. Zillions of little animals
[bacteria] are now yours."

All of a sudden, the world stopped. The
pets at the store were quiet. A caesura. For a
moment, Fred stopped breathing.

Fred had bought some
yellow snot for $100.

He wished that he had
parents there to comfort him.

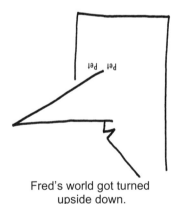

Fred's world got turned
upside down.

Tears ran down his cheeks.

small essay

Keeping Your Word

Fred did not ask for his money back. He had made an agreement with Coalback. Fred had promised that if Coalback did something (supply an animal), that Fred would do something (pay $100).

Coalback kept his part of the deal. And *Coalback had not lied.* This is important. If Coalback had lied (committed fraud), then Fred would not have to keep his word and go through with the sale.

If Fred says that he will meet you at 7:30, you can expect him to be there at 7:30. If Fred says that he will clean your bird's cage, it will be done. Fred keeps his word.

If Fred ever gets married, at the wedding he will promise to love and honor his wife as long as they both shall live. And you know that Fred will keep his word.

You get to pick your friends and pick your spouse (wife or husband). It's your choice. Pick people who: (1) don't lie, and (2) who keep their word. You will be a lot happier.

end of small essay

Fred headed into the restroom at **Pets—You Bet!** He put the handkerchief into the garbage and washed his hands.

He was too short to look into the mirror, but he realized that he should also wash his face.

Here's what a mirror looks like when
you are too short to look into it.
You don't see yourself.

While Fred was in the restroom, Coalback's sister came out of the backroom to talk to Coalback. She was angry.

He was counting his money: $20, $40, $60, $80, $100. (Fred had paid with twenty-dollar bills.) He said, "Look sister. We made a nice pile of money."

She said, "I heard everything. That kid is only four or five years old and you sold him your snotty handkerchief for a hundred dollars. The least you could have done was sold him one of our 39-cent goldfish. Goldfish don't breathe air. Now the kid is crying. Don't you care about his feelings?"

She paused. He said nothing. He put the money in his pocket and started to walk away.

She shouted, "Why did you do it? Why didn't you at least give him a stupid goldfish?"

He turned and said, "Frankly, my dear, snot is cheaper."

Your Turn to Play

1. If x is an even number, what can you say about x + 1?

2. Fill in the next three numbers in the sequence

      10, 20, 30, ___, ___, ___.

3. It is hard to define a **polygon** in English, but easy to see what a polygon is by example.

polygons   not polygons

Your question: Is every triangle a polygon?

```
....... ANSWERS .......
```

1. If x is an even number and you add one to it, you will always get an odd number.

$12 + 1 = 13$

$438 + 1 = 439$

$42,629,693,232 + 1 = 42,629,693,233$

2. 10, 20, 30, 40, 50, 60.

   A **sequence** is a bunch of numbers separated by commas.

3. Every triangle is a polygon.

Trying to define what a polygon is using English is tough. You take a bunch of straight sticks (line segments) and you join them at their ends (vertices), so there is exactly one hole in the middle. We will do a much better job defining polygons when we get to *Life of Fred: Geometry*.

<u>A Row of Practice.</u> *Do the whole row before you look at the answers.*

24	573	9 7	3	862
+ 89	− 7	+ 6	× 5	+ 568
113	566	22	15	1430

Chapter Eight
One in the Bag

Coalback was going to head into the backroom to put his $100 in a safe so that no one could steal it from him.

A police car rolled up to the front of the pet store.

Coalback saw the car and hid in the broom closet in the backroom, leaving his sister to face the police.

"Hi ma'am," he began. "This is just a routine call. Nothing to get excited about. We are just alerting everyone in the neighborhood. A couple just escaped from the county jail, which is four blocks from here. If you see anyone that is suspicious, please give us a call."

"Thank you officer," she said. "I sure will." She had the same crocodile smile that her brother had.

The policeman headed back to his car and drove off.

that crocodile smile

Fred came out of the restroom. He had missed everything.

✧ The police were gone.

✧ Coalback was in the broom closet.

✧ Coalback's sister relaxed her fake smile.

✧ Fred stood there with his little dot eyes looking like tiny red rubies (a simile).

"Look kid," she said. "My brother did you wrong." She scooped a goldfish out of one of the fish tanks, put it into a plastic bag with some water, and handed it to him. "Now, get out of here before he comes back, and I get into trouble."

Fred thanked her and headed out into the sunshine. He walked down the street with his new pet goldfish. He didn't feel like running. Crying can take some energy out of a person.

He had walked about a block when Coalback came running after him shouting,

"Give me back that goldfish! You didn't pay for it. It's mine."

Fred wasn't going to argue with someone who weighed 233 pounds more than he.

$$
\begin{array}{rl}
270 \text{ lbs.} & \text{Coalback's weight} \\
-\ \underline{37 \text{ lbs.}} & \text{Fred's weight} \\
233 \text{ lbs.} &
\end{array}
$$

Fred held up the plastic bag. Coalback grabbed it and yelled, "Stealing ain't right!"

The policeman was just coming out of the Daisy Donut store. He had been having an afternoon donut and telling the clerk at the store to watch out for a couple that had just escaped from the county jail.

He had heard the word *stealing* and walked over to investigate.

When he saw Coalback, he drew his gun and yelled, "Freeze!" He handcuffed Coalback.

Coalback smiled and asked, "How did you recognize me?"

"It was that orange shirt you are wearing."

Coalback had not noticed that the back of his shirt had some lettering on it. He thought that he had just managed to steal a free shirt from the jail before escaping.

If Coalback hadn't been so greedy about getting back that 39-cent goldfish, if he hadn't kept the jailhouse shirt that he stole, the policeman might not have caught him today.

Those who do evil are often unbelievably stupid.

Coalback's sister in her original disguise

In her new disguise

When Coalback's sister saw him get arrested, she headed into the restroom and changed her dress, put on more lipstick, added a necklace, and pulled the hair of her wig down over her face. Now, even her own brother wouldn't recognize her.

She put a sign on the door: "Closed for the day. Pets are resting." She turned out of the lights and hid in the backroom.

The policeman locked Coalback in the back of his patrol car and walked back to the pet store. Coalback had been arguing with Fred about a goldfish, so the policeman guessed that Coalback's sister might be connected with pets.

Here's what the pet store looks like from the sky. The policeman walked all the way

around the perimeter of the building. He looked in every window. He couldn't see anything except for some lights on the fish tanks that Coalback's sister had forgotten to turn off.

Your Turn to Play

1. Here is a diagram of the number of steps the policeman took as he walked around the building.

Each step was one yard long.

What is the length of the perimeter of this building?

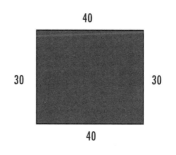

$$\begin{array}{r} 30 \\ 40 \\ 30 \\ +\ 40 \\ \hline \end{array}$$

·······ANSWERS·······

1.

$$30$$
$$40$$
$$30$$
$$+\ 40$$
$$140$$

He walked
140 yards.

Here is what you may have heard in your head as you worked this problem:

Always start with the column on the right. That's the ones column.

Adding up all those zeros is easy.

Then start on the tens column.

3 and 4 are 7.

And 3 more makes 10.

And 4 more makes 14.

A Row of Practice.

$$\begin{array}{r} 4 \\ 59 \\ +\ 7 \\ \hline 70 \end{array} \qquad \begin{array}{r} 27 \\ 6 \\ +\ 8 \\ \hline 41 \end{array}$$

Chapter Nine
Everything Felt Cleaner

She coughed. And coughed again. She couldn't stop coughing. It was a smoker's cough, and the policeman heard it.

He knew that dogs don't cough. Fish don't cough. He tapped on the window of the backroom and said, "Okay. I know you're in there. Come on out now."

ashtray mouth

Stupid cigarettes, she thought to herself. *Someday I gotta quit.*

Quiz Time!

Question: What is worse than when the doctor tells you that you have a bunch of black spots on your lung, and he has to cut out one of your lungs?
Answer: Wait a minute. I'm still trying to think of an answer.

Coalback's sister yelled, "I'm coming out."
A pair of handcuffs were waiting for her.

I've got the answer! The doctor tells you that you have a bunch of black spots on *both* of your lungs.

Moral: If you smoke cigarettes, remember to only suck the smoke into your least favorite lung.

After the policeman drove away with Coalback and his sister, Fred stood there with his goldfish in a plastic bag.

Everything felt cleaner when that evil pair was gone. Fred started walking back to his office. First north, and then west.

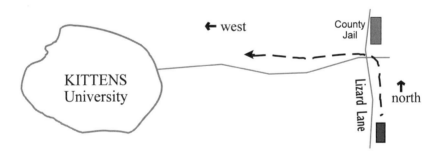

He thought about what he had learned in Sunday school about Heaven. With the Coalbacks gone, he understood that one of the nicest things will be that evil is gone. There will be no more lying, stealing, pain, or crying.

He sang a happy song to his goldfish as he walked down the road.

It was twenty minutes after three on a Saturday afternoon. Fred finally had a pet that both he and Kingie could enjoy. Everything was just ducky.*

3:20 p.m.

He carried the plastic bag very carefully. He didn't throw it up in the air. He didn't put it in his pocket.

Soon, he was at the Math building. He headed up the two flights of stairs, down the hallway, and into his office. Kingie was there doing his oil painting. He painted for hours each day. (In order to become really good at anything, you need to do lots of practice. That is why we have those Rows of Practice in this book.)

"We have a new pet!" Fred exclaimed. "And it fits our list of *Pets We Don't Want*."

----

* Ducky = excellent, wonderful. This has nothing to do with those web-footed swimming birds.

There is the comparative form of the word—duckier—but you don't hear it used that often. "Today is duckier than yesterday."

The comparative form of *tall* is *taller*. Of *bright* is *brighter*. Of *hot* is *hotter*. Of *good* is *better*. If English were as consistent as math, you could say *gooder*. But it isn't—so don't!

Fred placed the plastic bag on his desk. He

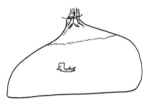

put three telephone books on his chair and sat
on them. Now he could see his new pet up close.

"You should see what he's doing," Fred told
Kingie. "He's swimming. This is the neatest*
goldfish in the whole world."

Kingie kept on painting. He wasn't
interested in some 39-cent goldfish.

Fred continued, "If I put him in a goldfish
show, I bet he would win first prize. I wonder
what I'll call him."

He hopped off his chair and got the
perfect—not "most perfect"—book from his
library: Prof. Eldwood's *Naming Your Pet Fish*,
1851.

In the chapter on pet sharks: Sammy
Shark, Sylvester Shark, and Silly Shark.

---

* Neat, neater, neatest. *Neater* is the comparative form. "My room is neater than your
room."

  Neatest is the **superlative** form. sue-PURR-la-tive

  Even *ducky* has a superlative form. This may be the only time in your life in
which you see this word written down. "This is the duckiest day of the year."

  Some adjectives don't have comparative and superlative forms. For example:
dead, excellent, impossible, and *unique.* If something is impossible, something else
can't be more impossible.

In the chapter on pet goldfish: Goldie Goldfish, Golly Goldfish, Gomer Goldfish, Gonzo Goldfish, and Gordy Goldfish.

Fred decided just to call him Fish for the time being.

Your Turn to Play

1. Find the perimeter of this rectangle.

$$7 \begin{array}{c} 16 \\ \boxed{} \end{array}$$

2. Find the perimeter of a triangle in which all three sides are 5 feet long. (This can be done without doing any addition!)

3. Find the next three numbers in the sequence
28, 26, 24, ___, ___, ___.

4. How long is it between 2:55 and 3:20?

5. If x is an odd number, what can you say about x + 2?

. . . . **ANSWERS** . . . .

1. If it's a rectangle, then the opposite sides have to be equal.

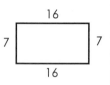

$$\begin{array}{r} 7 \\ \overset{2}{1}6 \\ 7 \\ + 16 \\ \hline 46 \end{array}$$

In your head, you would have 7 + 6 is 13.

Then 13 + 7 is 20.

Then 20 + 6 is 26.

Write down the 6 and carry the 2.

Then 2 + 1 + 1 = 4.

2. Instead of 5 + 5 + 5, you know that 3 × 5 = 15 feet, and you are done in one step.

3. 28, 26, 24, <u>22</u>, <u>20</u>, <u>18</u>.

4. From 2:55 to 3:00 is 5 minutes. } 25 minutes
   From 3:00 to 3:20 is 20 minutes.

5. If x were 7, then x + 2 would be 9.

   If x were 13, then x + 2 would be 15.

   If x were 101, then x + 2 would be 103.

Add 2 to any odd number, and you get an odd answer.

<u>A Row of Practice.</u>

$$\begin{array}{r} 36 \\ 7 \\ + 9 \\ \hline 52 \end{array} \qquad \begin{array}{r} 8 \\ 23 \\ + 8 \\ \hline 39 \end{array}$$

Chapter Ten
Just Swim Around

After about ten minutes, Fred's interest in the fish began to wane. He couldn't make it sit or fetch like a dog. It wouldn't come when he called it. If Fish were a cat, Fred could have picked him up and petted him. But Fish was a fish.

He pushed the plastic bag to a far corner of his desk. Fred's interest in Fish was like a waning moon (simile).

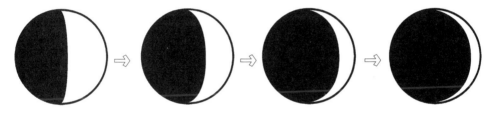

Fred wondered what Fish wanted to do when he grew up. He knew what the answer would be. Fish would just want to swim around all day long.

People are different. If you ask kids, "What do you want to do with your life?" you might get answers like:

❀ I want to install furnaces.

❀ I want to gather the world's largest collection of buffalo horns.

❇ I am going to write a book about having birthday parties.

❇ I want to grow acres of strawberries.

❇ I am going to make a movie about operating a bowling alley in South Carolina in 1928.

If you ask a fish, the only answer you will get is that it wants to swim around and eat.

Eat! Fred thought. *I forgot that I have to feed my goldfish.*

Fred looked in his desk. There were sandwiches, a jar of pickles, sticks of gum, a dried-out scoop of ice cream, a stick of spaghetti, an orange that had turned green with mold, and some jelly beans from Farmer's Nachos.

If he had put any of these into the plastic bag, he would probably have killed Fish.

Kingie had a suggestion: "Why don't you get some goldfish food? And while you are at it, you will also need to get a tank. Your pet won't survive very long in that little plastic bag."

"You are right, Kingie," Fred said. "Please take care of Fish till I come back." Fred headed out.

Kingie continued oil painting. He muttered to himself, "Take care of Fish? What is there to do? Am I supposed to tell Fish jokes to keep him entertained?" Kingie wasn't very excited about having a pet in the office.

Fred jogged over to the largest store in town: King KITTENS.

It had three main floors, and each floor was seven acres. $3 \times 7 = 21$. There were 21 acres of shopping space.

This was a huge store.* King KITTENS made $3 \times 7 = 21$ famous. When Fred was teaching the multiplication tables to his arithmetic class, he would just say, "King KITTENS" and the class would say $3 \times 7 = 21$.

Except Joe. He always said $7 \times 3 = 21$. He thought that King KITTENS had seven floors with three acres on each floor.

Your Turn to Play

central tower

1. Joe's girlfriend, Darlene, told Joe that King KITTENS has only three main floors.
    Joe said that he was looking at the central tower.
    "Those are windows, not acres!" Darlene shouted. "And it is only six floors tall."
    How many windows are in the central tower?
2. Find the next two numbers in the sequence
       3, 6, 9, 12, 15, 18, 21, ___, ___.
3. Most windows in most houses are what shape?
4. What do we call polygons with three sides?

---

* There are 43,560 square feet in one acre. If you took 20 homes, each 2,178 square feet, that would make an acre of living space.

·······ANSWERS·······

1. You could just count all the windows, but that would take a lot of time. 1, 2, 3, 4, 5, 6, 7, 8, 9, 10, 11, 12, 13, 14, 15, 16, 17, 18.

You could add up six 3s:

$$
\begin{array}{r}
3 \\
3 \\
3 \\
3 \\
3 \\
+\ 3 \\
\hline
18
\end{array}
$$

but that would take a lot of time.

Instead, $3 \times 6 = 18$ is much quicker.

2. 3, 6, 9, 12, 15, 18, 21, 24, 27

| 3 × 6 | | 3 × 7 |

3. Most windows are in the shape of rectangles.

4. Most people call polygons with three sides triangles. Joe calls them three-sided polygons.

A Row of Practice.

$$
\begin{array}{r}
35 \\
75 \\
+\ 48 \\
\hline
158
\end{array}
\qquad
\begin{array}{r}
62 \\
84 \\
+\ 8 \\
\hline
154
\end{array}
$$

Chapter Eleven
King KITTENS

When Fred entered King KITTENS, he was shocked. It was like pictures he had seen of giant churches in Europe. The only difference was what was being venerated*. At King KITTENS it was: auto tools, barbells, cat litter, . . . , and women's underwear.

inside a cathedral

"Here Comes Peter Cottontail" was being played over the loudspeakers to get people in the mood for shopping for Easter.

Time Out!
Biology Lesson

Those little brown things that bunnies lay are not chocolate eggs. Don't eat them!

King KITTENS was so large that they had buses running inside the store. That meant that people could shop longer before getting tired.

---

* Venerated = treating something with reverence, with awe, with honor, with respect.

They also had individual little cars that you could drive. Fred couldn't believe his eyes  when he saw a little lamb drive by in one of those cars. That lamb looked very familiar.

Fred spotted a sign.

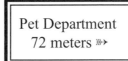

> Pet Department
> 72 meters »→

He knew he could walk a meter* in about two steps. So it would take him 72 + 72 steps to get to the pet department.

Instead of adding, we can multiply.

$$
\begin{array}{r}
72 \\
\times\ 2 \\
\hline
144
\end{array}
$$

We always start on the right.

2×2 is 4. Then $2 \times 7 = 14$.

He didn't need a car or a bus to walk 144 steps.

When he got to the pet department, he asked the clerk where the goldfish food was. She smiled and said, "It is 24 aisles down that way. You can't miss it." She looked very familiar.

---

* A meter was just a little longer than a yard. One meter is about 39 inches. One yard is 36 inches.

Fred started walking. It took him 3 seconds to walk past each aisle.* To walk past 24 aisles would take 24 + 24 + 24 seconds. Rather than add, we can muliply.

$$\begin{array}{r} \overset{1}{24} \\ \times\ \ 3 \\ \hline 72 \end{array}$$

We always start on the right.

$3 \times 4 = 12$. Write down the 2 and carry the one.

3×2 is 6, plus the one, equals 7.

In 72 seconds, Fred was at the goldfish food aisle.

It was one whole aisle of goldfish food— shelf after shelf. Fred had been expecting one or two choices. Instead, there were:

small, one-day packages,

one-ounce containers,

gold fish food from Argentina.

Pacific Ocean

Atlantic Ocean

Argentina is located in the southern part of South America.

It is considered a country of immigrants (like the United States, Canada, and Austrailia).

86% (86 out of each 100) of the population is originally from Europe.

---

* *Aisle*, *I'll*, and *isle* are homonyms—words that sound alike but have different meanings. An isle is a small island.

There were goldfish food products from lots of different countries. There was special food for happy goldfish and other food for lonely goldfish.

On one shelf was a giant container. One kilogram is a little more than two pounds.

Fred thought, *That must be for someone who owns a zillion goldfish.*

It was on sale for $27. Fred thought, *That's more than I spend on food for myself in a year.*

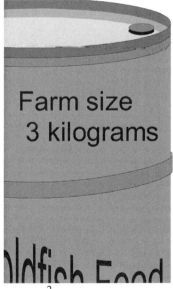

When he spotted the three-kilogram size, he didn't know what to think.

There was no price listed for the 3 kg size. Since it was three times larger than the 1 kg size, it probably cost about three times as much.

$$\begin{array}{r} \overset{2}{2}7 \\ \times\ \ 3 \\ \hline 81 \end{array}$$

Start on the right. Three times 7 is 21. Write down the 1 and carry the 2. Three times 2 is 6, plus 2, is 8. $81 for the big container.

Fred was overwhelmed with all the choices. A poster on the wall didn't help.

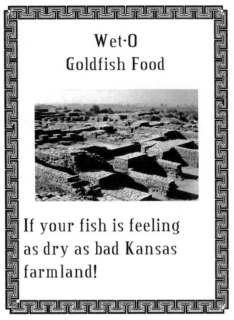

Wet·O
Goldfish Food

If your fish is feeling as dry as bad Kansas farmland!

That picture seemed very familiar to Fred. It looked a lot like Coalback's Fun Farm that he had visited. The clerk looked a lot like the agent at the ticket counter of **Dottie** airlines when he flew back home from Edgewood. The lamb in the car looked a lot like the lamb at *Little Lamb Farm*.

Part of growing older is that you have more memories—more things start to look familiar.

He had fond memories of the family at *Little Lamb Farm*: Mary and Roger and their nine children. His most unpleasant memory may have been of that duck that could never tell the truth. That was the duck in *Life of Fred: Apples* who told Fred, "You are a bowl of soup."

Fred spotted a sales associate who might be able to help him select the right goldfish food. That duck looked very familiar.

The duck said, "Goldfish food is what makes the sun come up every morning."

It was the duck who never told the truth.

Please first write down your answers to all of these questions. You will learn a lot less if you just read the questions and then read the answers.

Your Turn to Play

1. If the big container of goldfish food was $81 and the tax was $19, how much would be the total price?

2. If that duck said that he was 16 yards tall, how many feet would that be? (There are 3 feet in a yard. To convert yards to feet, you multiply by 3.)

3. What ocean touches Argentina? (You get extra points if you can remember without looking back at the map.)

4. Is this true? $5 + 4 \neq 17$

5. Horses do not lay eggs. People do not lay eggs. Bunnies do not lay eggs. What animals do lay eggs?

. . . . ANSWERS . . . .

1.
$$
\begin{array}{r}
\overset{1}{8}1 \\
+\ 19 \\
\hline
100
\end{array}
$$

You start on the right. $1 + 9 = 10$.
Write down the 0 and carry the 1.

The big container with the tax cost $100.

2.
$$
\begin{array}{r}
\overset{1}{1}6 \\
\times\ \ 3 \\
\hline
48
\end{array}
$$

You start on the right.
$3 \times 6 = 18$. Write down the 8 and carry the 1.

3 times 1 is 3, plus the 1, is 4.

The duck would be 48 feet tall.

3. The Atlantic ocean.

4. It is true that $5 + 4$ does not equal 17.

Atlantic Ocean

5. When I was about eight years old I owned a duck. My duck never told a lie. (She also never told the truth.) But she did lay eggs.

   If you want eggs, the place to look is female birds.

A Row of Practice.

$$
\begin{array}{cccc}
 & & 58 & \\
23 & 72 & 83 & 89 \\
\times\ 3 & -\ 8 & +\ 46 & \times\ 2 \\
\hline
69 & 64 & 187 & 178
\end{array}
$$

Chapter Twelve
Duck Tears

If Fred asked that duck what was the best goldfish food for his pet, the duck—who never told the truth—would point to the jar of rubber cement.

Could Fred ever find out what he wanted to know from a duck who always lied?

Fred had a brilliant idea. He asked, "What is the worst goldfish food? I want the one that is the lowest quality and the most expensive."

The duck was trapped. With tears in his eyes, he had to point to the best goldfish food.

Even the tears of that duck were a lie.
Ducks don't have lacrimal (LACK-reh-mel)
glands like humans do. The lacrimal glands
produce tears. If your baby brother was crying a
lot, you could say, "What lacrimation!" and tell
your friends that he is the world's best
lacrimator.

Fred selected a container of Acme Goldfish
Food and then asked the duck, "What is the way
that I *shouldn't* go to get to the fish tanks?"

The duck gave him the perfect directions.

Fred took the red bus to aisle 385,
transferred to the blue bus and rode to the third
elevator, which he took up to the second floor.
He turned left and walked 40 meters (which is a
little longer than 40 yards), and he was there.

King KITTENS presents . . .
The World's Largest Selection of
Aquariums

That sign was probably true. There were small
aquariums and large aquariums. There were
round ones and traditional ones where all the
faces were rectangles.

Some were made out of glass and others out of plastic.

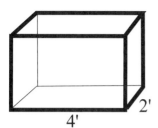

Fred spotted one that looked just perfect for his goldfish. The bottom measured four feet by two feet.

The area of the glass on the bottom was 8 square feet.

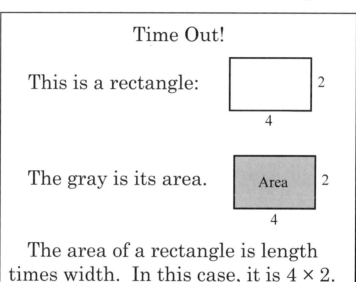

Time Out!

This is a rectangle:

The gray is its area.

The area of a rectangle is length times width. In this case, it is 4 × 2. Two times four is the same as 4 + 4, which is 8.

If we had taken the bottom of the aquarium and divided it into square feet, it would look like this. You can count them. There are 8 square feet.

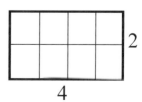

If you had a lawn that was four meters by two meters, then you would have to mow eight square meters of lawn every week. Area is really important in mowing lawns.

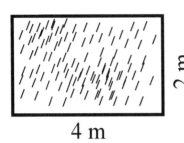

4 m

2 m

When you buy your dream house out in the countryside, one of the important things to know is how many acres of land you will own.

An acre is a measure of area. One acre equals 43,560 square feet.

In a city, there might be eight houses on each acre. Away from the city, there might be one house on 40 acres.

If you live in the city, you are closer to stores, to the public library, and to your neighbor's house.

If you live in the countryside, it is less noisy, more private, more peaceful, and there is more nature to enjoy.

Some people like the city. Some like the countryside.

Your Turn to Play

1. Here is the tank that Fred was looking at.

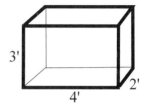

What is the area of each of the four sides of the tank?

2. The bottom of the tank measured
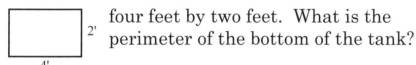
four feet by two feet. What is the perimeter of the bottom of the tank?

3. The perimeter matters if you are going to walk around the tank.

The area of glass matters if you are going to buy the glass to build a tank.

The volume of the tank matters if you are a fish who is going to swim in that tank.

Perimeter ⟫ length

Glass ⟫ area

Water in the tank ⟫ volume

To find the volume of the tank you multiply 3 times 4 and then multiply that answer times 2.

Volume = 3 × 4 × 2. Do it.

. . . . ANSWERS . . . .

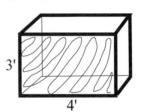

1. The front face of the tank

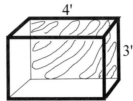

and the back face

are each 3 × 4, which is 12 square feet.

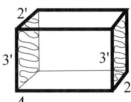

The side faces are each 3 × 2,
which is 6 square feet.

2.   The perimeter is   4

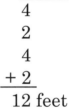

                                                 2
                                                 4
                                             + 2
                                       12 feet

3. To multiply 3 × 4 × 2, you first multiply 3 × 4.
3 × 4 = 12. Then you multiply 12 × 2.

                       12
                    × 2
               24 cubic feet

If perimeter were measured in *miles*, then area would be
in *square miles*, and volume would be in *cubic miles*.
Inches→*square inches*→*cubic inches*.
Meters→*square meters*→*cubic meters*.

Chapter Thirteen
Getting a Tank

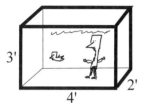

Fred liked that fish tank. Since he was three feet tall, it would be perfect. He could just fit inside if he wanted to play with his fish.

The only problem would be breathing.

Twenty-four cubic feet of water would give them plenty of room to play.

A cubic foot of water is seven and a half gallons of water.*

Seven and one-half is sometimes written $7\frac{1}{2}$.

If there are $7\frac{1}{2}$ gallons in one cubic foot, and Fred's tank has 24 cubic feet, he will have 24 times $7\frac{1}{2}$ gallons in his tank.

---

* Okay. That's not exactly true. One cubic foot is closer to 7.48052 gallons, but since readers haven't had decimals yet, we'll call it 7.5 gallons.

Time Out!

When we get to *Life of Fred: Fractions*, we'll learn how to multiply $7\frac{1}{2} \times 24$.

The answer will be 180 gallons.

That's a big aquarium!

A gallon of water weighs 8 pounds.

So 180 gallons would weigh 180×8. We are still working on the three times tables. We haven't gotten to multiplying by eight yet.

If you ask your older brother or sister, they can tell you that 180×8 is equal to 1,440.

Fill Fred's tank up and it would weigh 1,440 pounds. **HEAVY.**

Actually, a gallon of water doesn't weigh eight pounds. It is closer to $8\frac{1}{3}$ pounds, but since you haven't really studied fractions yet, we won't mention that.[*]

Fred thought that his 180-gallon tank was just right. At King KITTENS there were some

---

[*] Okay. A gallon of water doesn't weigh exactly eight and one-third pounds. It is closer to 8.3453 pounds, but since readers haven't had decimals yet, we'll just stick with eight pounds.

really big tanks—tanks that made Fred's tank look small.

One of the sales persons was just climbing out of one of the larger aquariums. She had been cleaning the inside of the aquarium.

"Hi!" she said. "May I help you select an aquarium?"

Fred thought briefly about getting that aquarium that she had been swimming in. He thought that that would be a nice treat for his pet.

Fred asked, "How much does that tank that you are coming out of cost?"

"It's $5,000," she answered.*

Fred did some quick figuring. His salary at KITTENS University is $500 per month. In 10 months, he would get $5,000.

Multiplying by Ten Is Easy

500 × 10 = 5,000
23 × 10 = 230
777 × 10 = 7,770
8 × 10 = 80
200 × 10 = 2,000

---

* With 4-digit numbers, you can write them either with or without a comma. It's nice to stay consistent. If you write 5,000 on one page, don't write 5000 on the next page.

55 × 10 = 550

12,345 × 10 = 123,450

1 × 10 = 10

8,080 × 10 = 80,800

Multiplying by 100 Is Harder

65 × 100 = 6,500

444 × 100 = 44,400

9 × 100 = 900

30 × 100 = 3,000

5,070 × 100 = 507,000

100 × 100 = 10,000

Joe Could Never Understand
How to Multiply by 1,000

(Joe never paid attention.)

43 × 1,000 = 43,000

8 × 1,000 = 8,000

992 × 1,000 = 992,000

50 × 1,000 = 50,000

17 × 1,000 = 17,000

6,666 × 1,000 = 6,666,000

23,456 × 1,000 = 23,456,000

Arithmetic class

Tuesday, February

dozen

Mickey came to class!!!!

Bow wow

for lunch

cookies
Sluice
candy

Fred thought, *Ten month's salary seems like a lot of money to pay for a fish tank. I love my little goldfish, but maybe there is a better use for $5,000.*

Your Turn to Play

1. Fill in the blank:

   To multiply by 10, you add one zero.

   To multiply by 100, you add __?__ zeros.

2. Make a guess. 53 × 1,000,000 = ?

3. In the previous chapter we computed that Fred's favorite fish tank would weigh 1,440 pounds when filled with water.

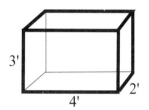

   How much would two of those tanks weigh when filled with water?

4. Would two tanks weigh more or less than a ton? (A ton is 2,000 pounds.)

5. Joe loves Bow Wow ice cream. Once he told Darlene that he could eat a ton of it.

   How many cartons would that be?

Bow Wow
Ice Cream

2 lbs.

·······ANSWERS·······

1. To multiply by 100, you add two zeros.

2. $53 \times 1,000,000 = 53,000,000$

In English, fifty-three times a million is equal to fifty-three million.

3. There are two ways you could find out how much two 1,440-pound tanks weigh.

First way: Add them
$$\begin{array}{r} 1440 \\ +\ 1440 \\ \hline 2880 \text{ pounds} \end{array}$$

Second way: Multiply
$$\begin{array}{r} 1440 \\ \times\quad 2 \\ \hline 2880 \text{ pounds} \end{array}$$

4. Two tanks weigh 2,880 pounds.

Since $2,880 > 2,000$, they would weigh more than a ton.

5. How many 2-pound cartons to equal 2,000 lbs.?

$2 \times 1,000 = 2,000$.

So one thousand cartons would weigh a ton.

Some readers may have been bothered by a dinosaur with roller skates, a baseball hat, and a camera on the front of a Bow Wow ice cream container. Joe thought that was funny.

Chapter Fourteen
Plastic Books for Fish

Fred pointed to the 180-gallon tank that he liked. He thought that would be the perfect size. It was four feet wide, three feet tall, and two feet deep.

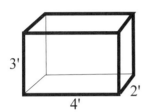

She said, "That is $600. You must have a lot of fish. Or are your fish really big?"

Fred said, "I only have one goldfish, and his name is Fish."

She smiled. "I think Fish would be very happy in a five-gallon tank. That would give him plenty of room to swim around."

Fred was worried. "Won't Fish get bored just swimming around in a small tank? Shouldn't I get him some plastic books to read?"

He knew that regular paper books wouldn't work well underwater.

She looked at little Fred and tried to explain in words that a five-year-old could understand, "You see, fish are not the same as people. They don't read books. They don't know that 3 × 8 = 24. They don't know that by the commutative law of multiplication that 8 × 3 is also equal to 24. They don't have a love of learning new things. They don't get bored."

Fred nodded. "You're right. We shouldn't anthropomorphize* fish."

She gasped. She didn't expect big words to come out of such a little kid.

Fred changed the subject. "Where can I get some plants to stick in my aquarium? I think that would look pretty."

Fred didn't say that the fish would enjoy them.

"On the third floor," she told him.

Fred took the fish food and the five-gallon aquarium and headed up the escalator. He was going to select some plants and then pay for everything. Then he was going to put his purchases in the KITTENS campus mail. They would get back to his office before he did.

KITTENS campus mail
Free delivery
Faster than email

---

* ANN-throw-peh-MORE-fize You anthropomorphize something if you pretend that it is like a human.

    We humans tend to like to anthropomorphize almost everything. Some baseball players lovingly talk to their mitts. Fred wanted to buy a book for his fish. Some people even anthropomorphize God and pretend that God is just an extra-big human.

    Anthropo means "concerning human beings." Anthropology is the study of everything about humans.

Then Fred realized that he didn't have any money. He put the fish food and the tank in a shopping cart and sat down to think.

Thought #1: *I could run back to my office and borrow some money from Kingie.*

Thought #2: *I could apply for a King KITTENS credit card.*

Thought #3: *I could come back another day when I had money and make my purchases.*

Thought #4: *I know!* Fred went to the mailbox and wrote a letter to Kingie:

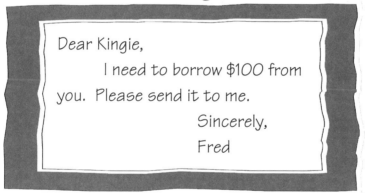

> Dear Kingie,
>   I need to borrow $100 from you. Please send it to me.
>   Sincerely,
>   Fred

He dropped it in the mailbox and a special light turned on. Student letter carriers rushed over to the box and got the mail and ran to deliver it.

As he walked back to the shopping cart, a student letter carrier rushed up and handed him . . .

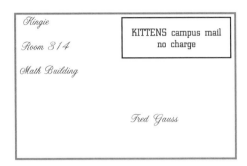

Fred always liked Kingie's handwriting.
The envelope contained five $20s.

$$20$$
$$\times \ 5$$
$$100$$

Either way works.
Take your choice.

$$
\begin{array}{r}
20 \\
20 \\
20 \\
20 \\
+\ 20 \\
\hline
100
\end{array}
$$

Fred pushed the shopping cart to the aisle marked "Plants for Aquariums."

As usual, King KITTENS had a huge inventory to choose from.

There was the 19¢ plastic plant.

And there was the $749 super plant collection, which even contained little plastic birds.

Your Turn to Play

1. Often, the best choice in life is somewhere in the middle. Not the cheapest. Not the most expensive.

Fred had to choose between a plastic plants and living plants. The $749 super plant collection had living plants gathered from around the world.

He decided to select a plastic plant. He was thinking, *Then it won't die if I forget to water it.*

Fred chose the $7.77 plant that had six shades of green in its leaves.

$7.77

"Nice looking plant you got there," the sales clerk said.

He looked very familiar.

He continued, "We got a sale on those plants right now. I can let you have three of them for the sale price of only $24."

Was that a good deal?

```
........ANSWER ........
```

1. Everyone (who has read this chapter) knows that three times eight is twenty-four.

So three $8 plants would cost $24.

But these plants are only $7.77.

It was not a good deal.

A Row of Practice.

$$
\begin{array}{cccc}
 & & 67 & \\
47 & 45 & 58 & 76 \\
\times\ 3 & -\ 8 & +\ 94 & \times\ 2 \\
\hline
141 & 37 & 219 & 152
\end{array}
$$

Chapter Fifteen
Three Plants

The more that Fred looked at that plastic plant with six shades of green in its leaves, the more he liked it. He decided to buy three of them, but not at the "sale price" of $28.

$7.77
$7.77
$7.77

He bought them one at a time.

$$\begin{array}{r} \overset{2}{}\overset{2}{}\,\,\,\\ 7.77 \\ 7.77 \\ +\ 7.77 \\ \hline \$23.31 \end{array}$$

Or you could multiply to find the answer.

$$\begin{array}{r} \overset{2}{}\overset{2}{}\,\,\\ 7.77 \\ \times\ \ \ \ 3 \\ \hline \$23.31 \end{array}$$

$7.77 means seven dollars and seventy-seven cents. The dot is called a **decimal point**.

The Acme Goldfish food was $2.07. The tank was $19. The three plants were $23.31. Fred wondered how much he had spent so far.

Fred could add that up in his head

$$\begin{array}{r} 2.07 \\ 19.00 \\ + \underline{23.31} \end{array}$$

but his real concern was *estimating* how much he would be spending. He just needed a rough idea. He wanted to make sure that the $100 that Kingie had sent him was enough.

Here was Fred's rough calculation:

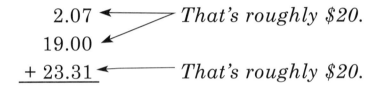

$$\begin{array}{r} 2.07 \\ 19.00 \\ + \underline{23.31} \end{array}$$

2.07 ←———— *That's roughly $20.*
19.00 ←
+ 23.31 ←———— *That's roughly $20.*

So, my total purchases are roughly $40.

When Fred bought three plants at $7.77, he knew that the total price would be somewhere between 3 × $7 and 3 × $8, because $7.77 is between $7 and $8.

Fred's total purchases so far were around $40. That meant that he had around $60 left.

$$\begin{array}{r} \$100 \\ - \ \underline{40} \\ \$60 \end{array}$$

Just because Fred had about $60 didn't mean that he had to spend it. His students, Joe and Darlene, are spendthrifts. If they have any cash, they would never think of saving it.

When Joe and Darlene get to be 59, they will be as broke as they are today at 19.

After Fred purchased the food, the tank, and the three plants, he put them in a campus mailbox. They would be waiting for him when he got back to his office.

Fred thought, *Is there anything else that Fish will need?* Some aquariums have heaters for the water, but you don't need that for goldfish. It's tropical fish that need heaters. Some aquariums have bubblers to add extra oxygen to the water, but since Fish was all alone in a five-gallon tank, he didn't need that.

Fred couldn't think of anything, so he headed home.

When he got back to his office, the fish food, the tank, and the plants were sitting on his desk right next to the plastic bag.

He said, "Hi!" to Fish and waved to him.
He wasn't sure whether Fish had heard him, but
the goldfish did wag his tail.

Fred looked at his desk and realized that if
he had bought that 180-gallon tank, it would
have covered his entire desktop. He would have
no place to work. He was glad that the clerk
had suggested the 5-gallon tank.

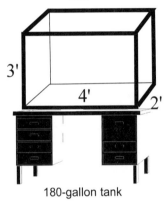
180-gallon tank

5-gallon tank

Fred was going to take the 5-gallon tank
down the hallway and fill it with water in the
restroom.

Water weighs about $8\frac{1}{3}$ pounds per gallon.
To estimate how much a tankful of water would
weigh, let's say it's 8 pounds per gallon.

Fred knew that $5 \times 8 = 40$.

5 gallons $\times$ 8 pounds/gallon = 40 pounds.

But Fred weighs 37 pounds. That tank
filled with water would weigh more than he

does. He needed to figure out another way to get that aquarium filled.

Your Turn to Play

1. If one package of Acme Goldfish food cost $2.07, roughly estimate how much 7 packages would cost.

2. If one 5-gallon tank cost $19, what would be the exact cost of 100 tanks?

3. Fred started out with $100. If he had spent $44, how much would he have left?

4. If two days from now will be Friday, what day was yesterday?

5. Find the next two numbers in the sequence
        4, 8, 12, 16, ___, ___

.......ANSWERS.......

1. $2.07 is pretty close to $2. Seven times two is the same as two times seven.

   $2 \times 7 = 14$

   > When Fred was teaching doubling, he pointed out that there are two seven-day weeks in a fortnight.

2. To multiply by 100, you add two zeros.

   $19 \times 100 = 1,900.$

   One hundred tanks would cost $1,900.

3.
   $$\begin{array}{r} 100 \\ - 44 \\ \hline 56 \end{array}$$
   He would have $56 left.

4. If two days from now is Friday, then today is Wednesday, and yesterday would be Tuesday.

5. This sequence is formed by adding 4 to get from one number to the next.

   4, 8, 12, 16, <u>20</u>, <u>24</u>

Chapter Sixteen
Filling the Tank

Fred thought of running a hose from the restroom to the fish tank on his desk. Then he wouldn't have to carry a tank filled with water down the hallway.

But he didn't own a hose.

He thought of taking the empty tank down to the restroom, filling it with water, and leaving it in the restroom.

But then he couldn't see Fish when he was working at his desk.

He thought of leaving Fish in the plastic sack.

But then Fish would probably die.

He thought of having Alexander fill up the tank in the restroom and carry it back to his office. Alexander is one of Fred's students. He is tall and strong.

But Alexander wasn't here.

He thought of getting a glass and filling it with water and carrying it back to the tank. If he did that a zillion times, he could fill up the tank.

But he didn't have that glass with the polka dots anymore. A two-year-old on the bus to Edgewood had taken that glass from him.

He thought of letting the water in the restroom splash on the floor until it flooded the whole third floor of the building including his office.

But that was silly. The water would run down the stairs.

He thought of ordering a 5-gallon jug of water from a water cooler company.

This is Saturday night, and we are closed till Monday morning.

But when he called the water cooler company, he only got a recorded message.

small essay
Real Thought

After Fred had realized that he couldn't carry a tank filled with water from the restroom back to his office, he has thought up seven different ways to try and solve his problem. None of them worked.

Is that bad? Heavens no. He is now seven steps closer to solving his problem.

Real thought takes a lot of work. It's much easier to do physical work than do hard thinking. That's one reason why physical work often pays a lot less than mental work.

end of small essay

He had an eighth thought. (*Eighth* is an ordinal number.) He headed to the restroom and took out his handkerchief.

It was one he had bought it at a thrift store. He liked the duck on it.

He wrote on the handkerchief.

and then

added

He wet the handkerchief in the restroom sink and put it into the campus mailbox that was right next to the sink. The light went on.

Four seconds later a student letter carrier returned the handkerchief to him.

He wet it again and mailed it again.

Soon the fish tank was filled with water.

Fred's handkerchief had suffered a little bit.

And so had the student volunteer letter carrier.

It was a good thing (for Fred) that campus mail is free.*

Fred raced down the hallway to his office. Everything was perfect. The tank was filled. The fish was swimming around happily in the plastic bag. The fish food hadn't been spilled. The plastic plants hadn't been stolen. Kingie was busy working on another oil painting. Fred

---

* In *Life of Fred: Pre-Algebra 2 with Economics* you will read about the Tragedy of the Commons. In short, Things that are free tend to get overused.

wasn't in the hospital. The heat was on in the building.

Most people miss those "perfect moments" in life. They would just continue dashing around.

Fred sat down at his desk. He looked at everything and smiled. He was grateful.

Your Turn to Play

1. {tank, fish} ∪ {tank, water}

∪ means "take the union of."

2. It was Saturday evening. Fred looked at the clock. What time was it?

3. Saturday is the seventh day of the week. Is 7th a cardinal or an ordinal number?

4. The cardinality of a set is the number of members in the set. The cardinality of {tank, fish} is 2.

The cardinality of {tank, water} is also equal to 2. What is the cardinality of {tank, fish} ∪ {tank, water}?

5. If it took the student letter carrier 4 seconds to make a wet handkerchief delivery, how many seconds would it take him to make 100 deliveries?

.... **ANSWERS** ....

1. {tank, fish} ∪ {tank, water} = {tank, fish, water}
The "spelling rule" for writing the members of a set in braces is that you do not repeat yourself. This would not be correct: {tank, tank, fish, water}.

2. You could say 5:45 or 5:45 p.m. or a quarter to six.

3. Seventh is an ordinal number. (Seven is a cardinal number.)

4. The cardinality of {tank, fish} ∪ {tank, water} is the same as the cardinality of {tank, fish, water}, which is equal to 3.

5. 4 × 100 = 400.   400 seconds

A Row of Practice

		39	
66	23	88	95
× 3	− 7	+ 36	× 2
198	16	163	190

Chapter Seventeen
In the Tank

Fred put the three plastic plants into the tank. He floated the plastic bag with Fish in it on the water. That allowed time for the water in the bag to change to the temperature of the water in the tank.

If Fred had just dumped Fish into the tank, the sudden change in temperature might have made Fish unhappy.

He didn't know for sure.

He was being careful.

He didn't want a dead goldfish.

Fred had placed the tank in the upper right hand corner of his desk.

He took a yardstick and made some measurements.

On a piece of paper he drew . . .

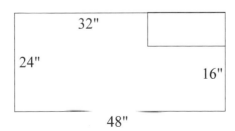

He knew that he didn't have to measure the dimensions of the tank. He could figure out those numbers.

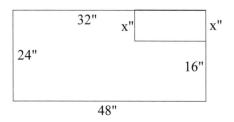

Let's call the short side of the tank x inches.

The left side of the desk is 24".
The right side of the desk is 16" + x".

$$24$$
$$-\ 16$$
$$8$$

The short side of the tank is 8".

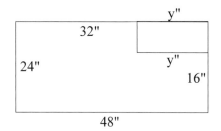

Let's call the long side of the tank y".

The side of the desk nearest Fred is 48".
The far side of the desk is 32" + y".

$$48$$
$$-\ 32$$
$$16$$

The long side of the tank is 16".

Fred now had all the measurements.

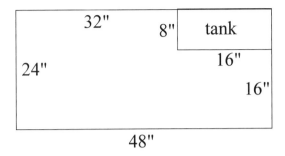

Enough time had passed. The temperature of the water in the bag was the same as the water in the tank.

Fred opened the plastic bag and let Fish swim into his new home.

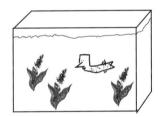

"Don't you think that Fish is pretty?" Fred asked Kingie. "He is so cute."

Kingie wasn't very interested in Fish. His passion was painting, not pets. He had just finished painting some flowers yellow ochre and was cleaning his brush. He was about to switch to cerulean (sah-RULE-lee-en) blue for work on the sky.

He made a caesura and went to look at Fred's new pet. He thought to himself, *At least I don't have to see Fred in the five-year-old's I-need-a-pet stage. I guess I should say something polite.*

Kingie said, "Yes. That is the cutest goldfish I have ever seen."* He then went back to his painting and opened a tube of cerulean blue.

Fred sat at his desk and watched Fish swim back and forth in the tank. Back and forth, back and forth, back and forth, back and forth, back and forth, back and forth, back and forth, back and forth, back and forth, back and forth, back and forth, back and forth.

Fish was happy in his tank.

Coalback wasn't happy. He was in his little cell at the county jail. It looked a little like Fred's fish tank.

He was angry. He paced back and forth in his cell. Back and forth, back and forth.

---

* Kingie was not lying when he used the superlative form *cutest*. He could have truthfully said that it was the *largest* goldfish he had ever seen. He could also have said that it was the *sweetest* goldfish that he had ever seen.

    He had never seen a goldfish before.

Your Turn to Play

1. Coalback would walk three steps and then have to turn around and walk three steps in the other direction. The cell was three paces long.

In an hour, Coalback walked the length of his cell 738 times. How many paces was that?

$$738 \times 3$$

2. Coalback's sister was in the women's part of the county jail. She just sat in a corner of her cell . . . and cried. She shed three tears each minute. How many tears did she shed in an hour?

3. Fred talked to his goldfish. This drove Kingie crazy. Kingie knew that goldfish can't understand English the way that dolls do.

But that didn't stop Fred. He told Fish about checkers, about bicycles, and about dancing.

These are things that fish are <u>not</u> interested in.

Fred talked about 54 topics each hour. How many topics did he cover in 3 hours?

·······ANSWERS·······

1. $\overset{1\ 2}{7\overset{}{3}8}$ 3 times 8 is 24. Write down the 4.

    × 3   Carry the 2.

    2214   3 times 3 is 9, plus the 2, equals 11.

    Write down the 1 and carry the 1.

    3 times 7 is 21, plus the 1, equals 22.

2. There are 60 minutes in an hour.

    If she shed 3 tears in a minute, she shed 60 times as many in an hour.

    60

    × 3

    180   She shed 180 tears in an hour.

3. If he talked about 54 topics each hour, he covered 3 times as many topics in 3 hours.

    54

    × 3

    162   He talked about 162 topics in 3 hours.

A Row of Practice

			69
57	94	86	43
+ 68	+ 28	+ 97	+ 39
125	122	183	151

114

Chapter Eighteen
What to Tell Your Fish

When some people get a new car, they wash it every day. When they get a new pizza maker, suddenly they want pizza for breakfast, lunch, and dinner.

Fred talked to his new pet for three hours. Fish just swam around in the tank while Fred explained why it is important to have a good collection of fountain pens and how to use  furniture polish on a coffee table.

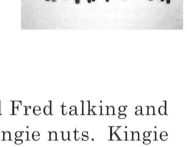

The goldfish didn't mind Fred talking and talking, but it was driving Kingie nuts. Kingie couldn't concentrate on doing his oil paintings when Fred was telling a goldfish the correct way to hold a spoon when you are eating soup.

Kingie washed his brushes and put away all his art equipment. He headed into his little fort in the corner of the room and closed the door.

As everyone knows, Kingie had a very small grand piano in the living room of his fort.

Playing the piano was a delightful escape. He wouldn't have to listen to Fred explaining to his fish the difference between downhill and cross-country skiing.

Kingie looked through his piano sheet music. He had his favorite composers alphabetized: Carl Friedrich Abel, Adolphe-Charles Adam, John Adams, Alexander Agricola, Jehan Alain, Isaac Albeniz, Tomaso Albinoni, Johann Georg Albrechtsberger, Georgio Allegri, William Alwyn, Gioachino Angelo, Jean-Henri D'Anglebert, George Antheil, Jacob Arcadelt, Thomas Augustine Arne, Malcolm Arnold, Kurt Atterberg, Daniel-François Auber, Milton Babbitt, Grazyna Bacewicz, Carl Philipp Emanuel Bach, Johann Christian Bach, Johann Sebastian Bach, Wilhelm Friedemann Bach, Samuel Barber, Ernst Bacon, Jean Barraqué, Béla Bartók, Arnold Bax, Ludwig Van Beethoven, Vincenzo Bellini, Alban Berg, Luciano Berio, Hector Berlioz, Leonard Bernstein, Franz Berwald, Heinrich Ignaz Biber, Gilles Binchois, Georges Bizet, Ernest Bloch, Luigi Boccherini, François-Adrien Boïeldieu, Arrigo Boïto, Guillaume Boni, Alexander Borodin, Pierre Boulez, William Boyce, Johannes Brahms, Havergal Brian, Frank Bridge, Benjamin Britten, Max Bruch, Anton Bruckner, Antoine Brumel, Gavin Bryars, John Bull, Antoine Busnoys, Ferruccio Busoni, Dietrich Buxtehude, William Byrd, Antonio De Cabezon, Giulio Caccini, John Cage, Antonio Caldara, Elliott Carter, Ferdinando Carulli, Robert Carver, Georgi Lvovitch Catoire, Emmanuel Chabrier, Gustave Charpentier, Marc-Antoine Charpentier, Ernest Chausson, Frédéric Chopin, Johannes Ciconia, Francesco Cilèa, Domenico Cimarosa, Aaron Copland, Arcangelo Corelli, Johannes Cornago, Pieter Cornet, William Cornysh, Michel Corrette, François Couperin, George Crumb, Bernhard Henrik Crusell, Luigi Dallapiccola, Franz Danzi, Peter Maxwell Davies, Claude Debussy, Michel Richard Delalande, Léo Delibes, Frederick Delius, Norman Dello Joio, David Diamond, Karl Ditters von Dittersdorf, Ernö Dohnányi, Gaetano Donizetti, John Dowland, Eustache Du Caurroy, Guillaume Dufay, Paul Dukas, Maurice Duruflé, Antonín Dvořák, Hanns Eisler, Edward Elgar, Georges Enesco, Ferenc Erkel, Manuel De Falla, Guido Alberto Fano, Johann Friederich Fasch, Gabriel Fauré, Robert Fayrfax, Morton Feldman, Brian Ferneyhough, John Field, Gerald Finzi, Johann Caspar Fischer, Arthur Foote, César Franck, Benjamin Frankel, Girolamo Frescobaldi, Johann Jakob Froberger, Walter Frye, Giovanni, Gilbert & Sullivan, Gabrieli, Niels Wilhelm Gade, Geminiani, George Gershwin, Don Carlo Gesualdo, Orlando Gibbons, Alberto Ginastera, Umberto Giordano, Mauro Giuliani, Philip Glass, Alexander Glazunov, Reinhold Gliére, Mikhail Glinka, Christoph Willibald Gluck, Johann Gottlieb Goldberg, Nicholas Gombert, Henryk Górecki, Louis Moreau Gottschalk, Morton Gould, Charles Gounod, Percy Aldridge Grainger, Enrique Granados, Edvard Grieg, Charles Tomlinson Griffes, Nicolas De Grigny, Sofia Gubaidulina, George Frideric Handel, Howard Hanson, Roy Harris, Lou Harrison, Karl Amadeus Hartmann, Johann Adolf Hasse, Franz Joseph Haydn, John Hebden, Pantaleon Hebenstreit, Johann David Heinichen, Hans Werner Henze, Hildegard von Bingen, Paul Hindemith, Lee Hoiby, Gustav Holst, Arthur Honegger, Alan Hovhaness, Herbert Howells, Johann Nepomuk Hummel, Engelbert Humperdinck, Jacques Ibert, Vincent D'Indy, Heinrich Isaac, Charles Ives, etc.

Kingie played a piece by Haydn (HIDE-n) and then one by Chopin (SHOW-pan). For three hours,

Fred talked, the fish swam, and Kingie was lost in the delight of great music. Everybody was happy.

Kingie played nine pieces each hour. In three hours, he played 27 pieces.

$$3 \times 9 = 27$$

This is the last multiplication fact for the three-times tables.

Time Out!

Did you know that learning the three times tables is one of the hardest of the times tables to learn?

You learned seven multiplication facts in this book:

$3 \times 3 = 9$
$3 \times 4 = 12$
$3 \times 5 = 15$
$3 \times 6 = 18$
$3 \times 7 = 21$
$3 \times 8 = 24$
$3 \times 9 = 27$

Seven facts is a lot easier than memorizing all the composers on the previous page!

When you get to learning the eight times tables, there will be only two facts to learn: $8 \times 8 = 64$ and $8 \times 9 = 72$. Life gets easier. You won't have to learn $8 \times 3 = 24$. You already know that since $3 \times 8 = 24$.

The goldfish kept swimming around in the tank. He didn't seem to be getting sleepy at all. But Fred was getting tuckered. It was nearly nine o'clock. Fred rubbed his eyes.

As he got up, he said to Fish, "I'll tell you more about everything tomorrow."

Fred headed down the hallway to the restroom. He found his handkerchief on the sink. He folded it and put it in his pocket. It was probably the cleanest handkerchief in all of Kansas.

In order to practice the metric system, he measured out 20 centimeters of floss.* As he flossed his deciduous teeth (baby teeth), he played with the numbers: *If 20 cm is about 8 inches, then 10 cm must be about 4 inches.*

If 10 cm is about 4 inches, then 5 cm must be about 2 inches.

---

* 20 cm is about 8 inches. The abbreviation for centimeter is cm. The abbreviation can either be written as cm. or as cm. Wait! Help! English is so hard. What I want to say is that you can write *cm* without a period, or you can write *cm.*

I wish that it was okay in English to write: Centimeter can be abbreviated as cm.. But two dots at the end of a sentence is not permitted.

Let me try again.

Cm. can be used as an abbreviation for centimeter and so can cm.

No. That doesn't work.

Either cm or cm. can be used as an abbreviation for centimeter. Yes!

He took out a tube of his favorite toothpaste and applied a dab to his toothbrush.

The toothpaste was not made in Kansas, but in the country of Freedonia. Why didn't Fred buy the American toothpaste and "save American jobs"?

The answer is that there are many cases in which *buying the foreign product will improve the American standard of living* including higher paying American jobs and more money in our pockets.

It is all explained (and proved) in *Life of Fred: Pre-Algebra 2 with Economics*, but it requires that you know about fractions such as $\frac{1}{3}$ and $\frac{5}{8}$ in order to understand the proof.

Your Turn to Play

1. If Fred could brush one tooth in 5 seconds, how long would it take him to brush 10 teeth?

2. How long would it take him to brush his 20 teeth?

3. What is $3 \times 3 \times 3$?

4. Draw a circle and color in $\frac{1}{2}$ of it.

. . . . ANSWERS . . . .

1. It would take him 10 times as long.

Ten times 5 seconds is 50 seconds. $5 \times 10 = 50$

2. If it took him 50 seconds to brush 10 teeth, it would take him twice as long to brush 20 teeth.

$50 \times 2 = 100$ seconds.

$$\begin{array}{r} 50 \\ \times\ 2 \\ \hline 100 \end{array}$$

3. $3 \times 3 \times 3 = 9 \times 3 = 27$

4.

A Row of Practice.

$$\begin{array}{cccc}
 & & 52 & \\
59 & 406 & 77 & 87 \\
\times\ 3 & -\ 7 & +93 & \times\ 2 \\
\hline
177 & 399 & 222 & 174
\end{array}$$

Chapter Nineteen
End of the Day

Fred put away his toothbrush and toothpaste. He washed his face, being careful not to cut his hands on the point of his nose.

He looked in the mirror, but he was still a bit short. Most of the teachers at KITTENS University are taller than three feet.

He looked in vain for some hair on his head. *I'm five years old*, he thought to himself. *My head looks as bald as some babies who are two months old.*

And where are my ears?

And my nose. I'm the only one I know who can use his nose as a letter opener.

And my head. It looks like the north end of Texas.

Texas

But what most concerned Fred about his physical appearance was his height. He had just turned five last month and he was only 36 inches tall.

He had looked it up on the Internet. The average two-and-a-half-year-old was 36 inches tall.

He found this bar graph for boys at age 5:

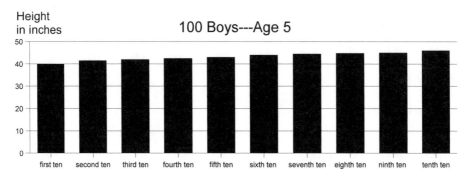

The first ten boys out of a hundred had an average height of 40 inches. The tallest ten boys had an average height of 46 inches.

And I'm 36 inches tall!

Since Fred was 3 feet tall and since 1 foot = 12"

$$\begin{array}{r} 12 \\ \times\ 3 \\ \hline 36 \end{array}$$

Fred is 36" tall.

Fred was starting to feel sad. That can happen when you think about negative things.

He walked down the hallway toward his office. He passed the nine vending machines (four on the left and five on the right).

Fred didn't eat very often. When he did eat, it was usually from these machines. He had no parents to teach him that a diet of candy, donuts, and Sluice doesn't provide the protein and calcium needed for growth.

Protein helps grow muscles.

Calcium helps grow bones.

Fred entered his office. Kingie's fort was dark and quiet. Fish was still swimming around in his tank.

Fred changed into his pajamas and unrolled his sleeping bag. He picked out three books from his library.

He turned off the room light so Fish could sleep and put a little lamp under the desk so that he could read.

It had been a long day. In the morning he had gotten the urge to do some farming and had visited two farms. He had met Mary and Roger and their nine kids.

In the afternoon he had turned pet crazy. After discussing which pets were acceptable to Kingie, he visited the grand opening of Pets—You Bet! and came home with a lovely goldfish.

He had so much to be happy about: his new pet, his artistic doll Kingie, his health, his home at KITTENS University, his friends, and his job where he could teach his favorite subject.

He smiled and snuggled down into his sleeping bag. He was too tired to read. He said a prayer of thankfulness for all the good things in his life, turned out the light, and headed off to sleep.

Index

> If you would like to
> learn more about
> books written about
> Fred . . .
>
> FredGauss.com

After you have finished the *Life of Fred Elementary Series,* there are 14 hardback *Life of Fred* books that will take you all the way up into your third year of college. (for details, see the next page)

You are not done then!

It won't be long after that before you are opening up the first book in the series, *Life of Fred: Apples,* again. This time to read it to your kids.

Celebrate that good news!

Polka Dot Publishing

We are proud of our low prices.

Life of Fred: Fractions	$19
Life of Fred: Decimals and Percents	$19
Life of Fred: Pre-Algebra 1 with Biology	$29
Life of Fred: Pre-Algebra 2 with Economics	$29
Life of Fred: Beginning Algebra	$29
Fred's Home Companion: Beginning Algebra	$14
Life of Fred: Advanced Algebra	$29
Fred's Home Companion: Advanced Algebra	$14
Life of Fred: Geometry	$39
answer key *Life of Fred: Geometry* (paper)	$6
Life of Fred: Trigonometry	$29
Fred's Home Companion: Trigonometry	$14

Two years of college calculus.

Life of Fred: Calculus	$39
answer key *Life of Fred: Calculus* (paper)	$6

A year of college statistics.

Life of Fred: Statistics	$39
answer key *Life of Fred: Statistics* (paper)	$6

Linear algebra is a math course that is required of almost all math majors in college. It is usually studied after calculus.

Life of Fred: Linear Algebra	$49
answer key *Life of Fred: Linear Algebra* (paper)	$6

Order through our website: PolkaDotPublishing.com